Ripples of Hope

Jimi Cook

TRILOGY CHRISTIAN PUBLISHING

Tustin, CA

Acknowledgements

My greatest thanks go to God for blessing me with an amazing family, my amazing wife, Cristi, friends who have become family, and incredible opportunities and experiences that have enriched my life beyond my wildest dreams. These are surely my greatest earthly treasures, which bring me so much joy and keep my flame of hope burning bright.

Special thanks to Rita for being an incredible writing coach and providing the foreword for this book, to Thato for the perfect image for the front cover, and to Kylee, Matt, Grant, Stacie, Ned, and Kourtney for their input and edits to help me tell these stories better. And, special thanks to the people who took the photographs I have included in this book. Whether they intended to or not, and whether they knew it or not, their pictures are telling some amazing stories that have changed lives for the better, changed our world for the better, and I hope will change your life for the better as well.

This book is dedicated to all of the people whose stories I get to tell in it. To me, their stories, and more importantly, their lives modeled the most essential character traits that I think each of us needs to ingrain in ourselves in order to live and love well. I will forever be grateful for them and their influences on me. Each of them "created a splash" that had a ripple effect on me, and I believe their stories will impact your life too. Let their ripples of hope, kindness, generosity, compassion, humility, grit, courage, gratitude, empathy, joy, forgiveness, and love touch your heart and soul...again and again and again, and then, create some ripples of your own, send them out, and see them build into a wave of change

JIMI COOK

**All proceeds from sales of this book directly support Be The Change Volunteers+.

+*Be The Change Volunteers* (BTCV) is a US-based development aid non-profit organization dedicated to creating better education opportunities worldwide. http://www.bethechangevolunteers.org

iv

Foreword

For many of us, the news headlines on any given day are enough to make us recoil in deep despair and an overwhelming sense of helplessness. Maybe you also sometimes find yourself typing "good news" into a search engine, hoping for hope, as I did today. I learned that firefighters have rescued a bucket of ducklings, engineers have developed solar panels that generate electricity at night, and a large study in the UK shows that the pandemic has made people kinder. Then I opened *Ripples of Hope*, and within its pages I found a treasure trove of good news. A compendium of inspiring vignettes that are part love-letter / part blueprint for how to combat despair and helplessness by giving of ourselves, this book promises that even the smallest acts of kindness can have exponential ripple effects that can—and do—change the world.

In keeping with the book's ode-like appreciation for some of the every-day superheroes who have graced Jimi's life, it makes sense to tell you how I came to know Jimi. When my frisbee-fetching therapy dog needed surgery to repair a ruptured ligament, I decided that the minimally invasive surgery Jimi invented would be best for him, but I couldn't find a surgeon in the Boston area who knew how to do it. I emailed Jimi, not really expecting to hear back, and within minutes, there was a message from him in my inbox. When I asked him what the odds were that he might be making a trip from Missouri to Massachusetts in the near future, I certainly didn't expect him to say that he would be in Boston in a matter of weeks, let alone to joyfully agree to perform my dog's surgery at a hospital ten minutes from my house. Only later did I incidentally discover that it had been Jimi's birthday on the day he operated on my pup and that he'd come to Boston to celebrate with friends. Even after I got to know Jimi and count myself among his friends, I never would have dreamed that he would come back years later to operate on my other dog in the middle of a pandemic for which we didn't yet have a vaccine.

At the heart of this book, I think that's what you'll find: people whose goodness and generosity consistently transcend expectations and, in doing so, make the seemingly impossible possible. Filled with humor, humility, and, as its title declares, hope, this book is a meditation on the qualities that propel us to be our best selves, an invitation to inhabit those qualities, and a celebration of the triumphs of the human spirit. It's the kind of book that leaves you feeling stronger than when you opened it, one to return to again and again, one to give to those we love.

Rita Zoey Chin
Author of the best-selling memoir,
Let the Tornado Come

Preface

In a world that seems so divided and divisive, and often seems devoid of hope, we need to look for those courageous women and men, boys and girls who are not following the polarizing crowds. We need to find trailblazers who are making paths and leaving trails of hope, kindness, generosity, compassion, humility, grit, courage, gratitude, empathy, joy, forgiveness, and love. They may not make a splash on the world's stages, but they sure can make a splash in the world – and in your life.

Mister Rogers said, "When I was a boy and I would see scary things in the news, my mother would say to me, 'Look for the helpers. You will always find people who are helping.'"

I have been blessed to have a number of helpers build into my journey, model these life-giving traits for me, and wash over me with their ripple effects in ways that have changed my life for the better. My wish is for everyone to find the helpers, and so I have tried to extend their ripples of hope by sharing their stories in this book.

How do you find the helpers, the changers, the ripple-makers? Travel to the ends of the earth? Rub elbows with the rich and the famous? Run toward the burning building? I think it is much simpler than that. I think you just need to 'be present.' Engage in conversation. Don't think about what you are going to say next, think about what the other person is saying right now. Take it in. Deep into your heart and soul. And, let silence have its purpose and impact. Be determined to learn something from every conversation. Be committed to following up on things – even the little things. Hold a hug for an extra moment. Don't ask someone how they are doing without actually waiting to hear the answer. Take joy in others' joy. Feel sorrow in others' sorrow. Walk with them through the storm – carry them when needed. Assume the best – more than once. Always find hope – even if it is only the smallest ripple, it is there – in a child's curiosity, a friend's smile, a sister's phone call, a brother's helping hand, a parent's question, and a grandparent's warm embrace. And the beautiful thing about hope is that once you find it, you are able to give it to others and you immediately have even more of your own. The ripple has started, and it will grow and return and grow and return – creating waves of resiliency, resolution, and resolve and a rising tide of passion that lifts you to say and feel and do things that you didn't know were even possible. For "you cannot swim for new horizons until you have courage to lose sight of the shore." (William Faulkner)

So, find hope. Practice kindness, generosity, and compassion. Be humble, gritty, and courageous. Show gratitude and empathy. Then, I can promise you that you will have joy, forgiveness, and love wash over you – and all those around you – again and again and again...

Contents

CHAPTER 1

HOPE—Sam

The new dawn blooms as we free it. For there is always light, if only we're brave enough to see it, if only we're brave enough to be it.

~Amanda Gorman

I reached into the back seat of the Malawian cab and lifted Sam out of the car and carried him up to the couch on the veranda of the guesthouse. I had known Sam for five years by this point and while he had always been thin and slight from having polio as a young child, this was the weakest I had ever seen him. I was really, really worried as I set his frail seventeen-year-old body on the couch next to me for our visit, and my worry intensified as I looked at our Malawian contact's face and saw an unmistakable look of dread and sorrow. I could not prevent the thought that this might be the last time I ever got to be with Sam from overwhelming my mind – and heart.

Each of us spoke only a few words of each other's language and although we had our contact to interpret, I started out just speaking English directly to him. I propped him up on the couch so that he looked more comfortable and kneeled in front of him so that we were face-to-face, mustered a smile, and said, "Gosh, it is so good to see you Sam-my-man, how are you?" As soon as the words 'Sam-my-man' left my lips, that incredible smile of his burst onto his face and transported me back to the first time I got to experience its radiant power.

We were working in a small village outside of Lilongwe, helping the community build a library and restore classrooms on the primary and secondary school campus. During a lunch break, we were playing soccer with the kids, and I noticed a young boy in a wheelchair sitting on the sidelines watching all the other kids play with obvious longing in his eyes. I asked the other kids who he was, and they said, "Sam, he is sick."

I said, "Do you think he wants to come play?"

They replied, "He can't play, he is in the chair."

I said, "Of course he can," and walked over to talk to him.

I used a combination of words, gestures, and antics to let him know he could play if he wanted to, and I would be his teammate and push his chair. He was very hesitant, and the other kids just stood and watched initially, which did not make for much of a game; but Sam and I just went ahead and took the ball– me pushing his chair, him reaching down and pushing the ball with his hand—and scored. That got all the kids to play and in a very short time it was full-on competitive soccer and I promise you, no one was giving Sam any breaks or treating him 'special'—just like he wanted it and just like it should be.

Well, for better or worse, I am a very competitive person, and I was quickly caught up in the game, including getting into flat-out sprints pushing Sam's chair so he could get the ball and make a play. During one of these runs, the smallest player on the field, who was only five or six years old, jumped in front of us to try to get the ball. Well, I slammed on the brakes Fred-Flintstone-style, and you can guess what happened. Sam literally went flying out of the chair like a dock-diving dog and hit the dusty Malawian ground with a thud and a skid.

Time stopped.

I was mortified, scared, and worried. Sam was face-down in the dirt, initially not moving at all.

As I rushed over to him, I could see his body shaking and I was sure that he was crying, or worse. I got to him and turned him over as the crowd of kids gathered around us. As I started to see the front of his body, I noted two scraped and bleeding knees, two scraped and bleeding elbows, a T-shirt covered in dirt, and a very dusty and dirty face with the biggest smile you have ever seen and the most joyous laugh you have ever heard. To this day, it was one of the most beautiful—and relieving—things I have ever seen.

Sam was just one of the kids—playing soccer, getting scraped up, and getting right back out there. Which he did and continued to do from that day forward. I gave him the nickname, 'Sam-my-man,' which always brought that huge smile to his face. We started letting the kids be his teammate, which made me a bit jealous, but made it sustainable. And each year we came back to Malawi, Sam and I would get in a game or two—and we always (well, almost always) won!

We learned that Sam was an excellent student and had a dream of going to university and being a radio broadcaster. Even though the village school was not set up at all to handle a student in a wheelchair, Sam found a way to make it there every day, get up the classroom steps with the help of friends, wheel his chair to the front row, and excel! Learning about the physical hurdles he was dealing with, we immediately revised the plans for the multi-year renovation projects at his school. We included ramps for every classroom and made sure they were wide enough and long enough to work for Sam – and Sam helped build every one of them.

Reliving these wonderful memories buoyed my spirit.

I think maybe Sam was reliving our adventures too because when I focused back in on the current-day moment, he gave a little chuckle and then with great effort, slowly and mechanically patted the couch next to him, indicating that he wanted me to sit right beside him. I immediately did so and put my arm around him as we then shifted to talking through our interpreter.

Sam, speaking very quietly and with uncharacteristic and worrisome labored effort, started the conversation, "How many schools now?"

"Ah, BTCV+ is up to 37 projects completed now with more than 6,000 students enrolled."

"Mmmm, that's good, I am proud of you."

"What about you, Sam, how is school for you?"

"I am still planning for varsity (university) – it is still my dream."

"That's awesome, Sam, now I am the one who is proud! How is your health now? I am concerned about you. Is there something we can do to help you get stronger?"

Then, Sam said something so poignant and profound, which I will never forget and never lose sight of even in my darkest moments. His voice got strong as he turned his gaze toward me and focused his deep brown eyes on mine, and said, ***"There are times when the flame of hope flickers and I can only just make out its light, but it never goes fully dark, and I will not lose it from my view."***

And then, that big, beautiful smile lit up his face and lit up my soul.

It was so profound and impactful, that our interpreter paused for a long moment as I did, both of us wanting to let the meaning and feeling of those words and that smile wash over us again and again and again.

We talked for a bit longer about the project we just completed, plans for more projects, and things going on in the US. Then, it was time for Sam to get back to his home. I picked him up again, put him back in the cab, gave him a long embrace that he fully leaned into, gave him a kiss on the forehead, and shut the door. I did not know for sure if I was shutting the door and waving good-bye to Sam for the last time as the cab drove away, but I knew for sure that Sam would be okay. He had purpose, direction, and passion. He had hope.

We came back to Sam's village two years later and I went to visit him at his house. He was nineteen years old then. Harry (one of our Malawian partners) and I looked all around the village and could not find him. I was getting worried. Finally, Harry found his older sister, whom I had never met. Harry told her who we were and that I was hoping to see Sam. She immediately burst into tears and fell into me with a strong embrace, which was not a cultural norm and in fact would be considered taboo by some. Now, I was really worried. But my fears turned to unequivocal elation when Harry translated to me that Sam was at university, first in his class, and was running the campus radio station! The joy and pride I feel for Sam are unexplainable. I just keep thinking—he made it! He did it! And he has inspired me and so many others along the way! And I did get to see him the next day. He looked handsome, smart, confident, and strong! Hope burned bright in his eyes and in his smile and washed over me in a beautiful wave of pure joy.

We will all have times when the flame of hope flickers and we feel that we are caught in an inescapable darkness. When those times come, let Sam's words wash over you again and again and again, and look as long and as far as it takes to bring that flicker of hope back into view – it is always there, somewhere, *if only we're brave enough to see it, if only we're brave enough to be it* – like Sam-my-man.

Portions of this chapter were adapted from, *Hand Delivered Hope*, Trilogy 2020
+*Be The Change Volunteers* (BTCV) is a US-based development aid non-profit organization dedicated to creating better education opportunities worldwide. http://www.bethechangevolunteers.org

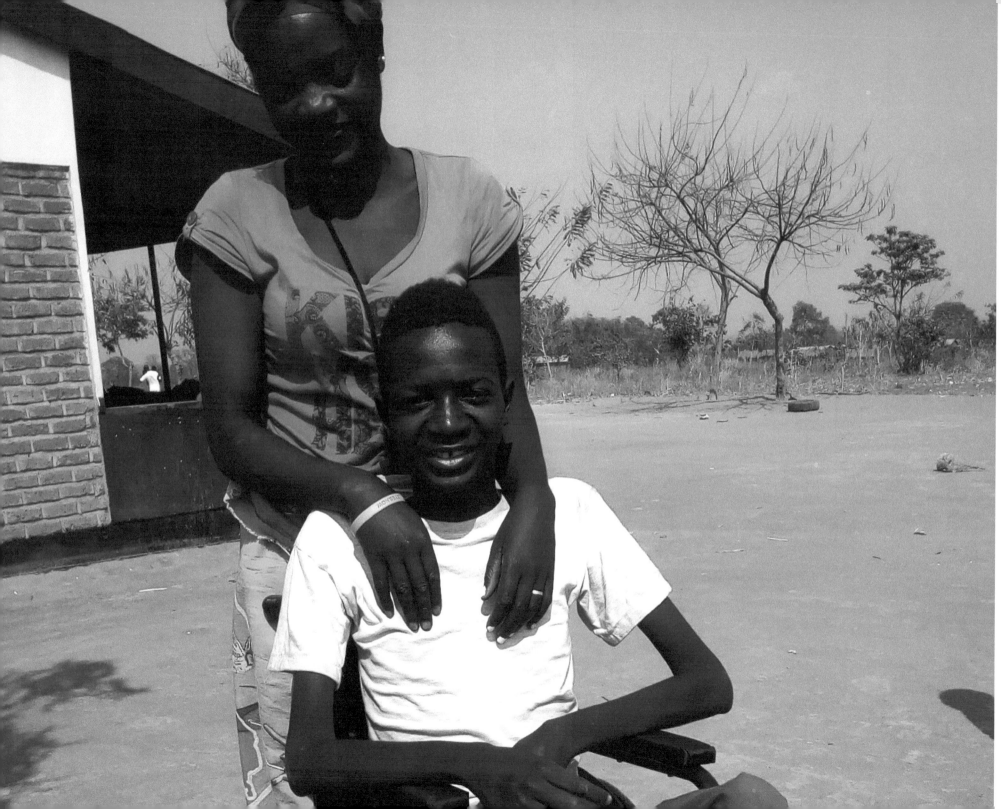

CHAPTER 2

KINDNESS—Jake

There's no such thing as a small act of kindness. Every act creates a ripple with no logical end.

~Scott Adams

We were in the middle of the very, very hot and very, very humid Peruvian jungle hand-mixing and pouring concrete – yards and yards and yards of concrete - for the El Chino High School classroom pilings and floor. We were working with this amazing community on the fifth phase of a whole-campus school-building project. It was extreme, heavy labor with a strict deadline to finish by sundown based on the way the forms were set up, the availability of workers, and the ever-present threat of a torrential rainstorm (like we experienced the previous day). The workforce was comprised of a team of eighteen volunteers from the US and the majority of the members of the Chino community.

El Chino is a tiny little jungle village set on the very remote Tahuayo tributary of the Amazon River and is dependent on subsistence farming and fishing for survival. This little village is incredible in so many ways, including the community engagement and commitment to education for their kids. For each project, community leaders put a work schedule in place such that each family contributed to the work, and on concrete days, this meant all hands on deck. The Chino men were mixing and shoveling concrete as fast as is humanly possible – sometimes even progressing to a superhuman pace. The Chino women were hauling water from the river to keep this incredible pace going. The local kids – from five years old to early teens – were bringing the sand over to the pile in buckets and bags and wheelbarrows. The volunteers were carrying bags of cement and shoveling sand for the mixing, and then, acting as the 'bucket brigade' to haul the concrete from the mix site to the classroom in five-gallon buckets. It felt and, I think if anyone would have been standing around not working, looked like one of those sped-up videos or cartoons where entire buildings are built in just a few minutes by a team of flitting, darting, and dashing humans with seemingly robotic capabilities.

Jake, one of our team members, was a fifteen-year-old American boy – *need I say more?* – primarily there at his father's prodding, or so I thought. But honestly, I could not have been more wrong in applying that stereotype or in thinking that Jake was not there for all the right reasons. Jake worked his butt off from day one of the project, doing any and every job asked of him well and with a smile on his face. But the thing I loved most about watching Jake on this build was how he 'got it' – he understood that building the school was important, but what was most important was building relationships. I saw him engage with Chino kids, moms, dads, grandmas, and grandpas – in the work and in the fun. I saw him help teammates, encourage teammates, and listen to teammates. I saw him willingly and enthusiastically work with his dad and the other 'old guys' on the team. I saw him pose and smile for pictures.

Then, I saw something life changing.

Jake was frenetically shoveling sand to keep up with the multifaceted assembly line that was working at record speed to try to get everything done before dark. It was an intricate and well-oiled process that required hard work with everyone keeping up with the crazy pace. At the height of this organized chaos, I looked over from where I was heaving bucket after bucket of cement up to my teammates on the classroom platform to catch sight of a tiny little girl from the community trying to carry a bucket of sand over to the giant mixing pile. Now this bucket was far too big for her, but she was absolutely determined to do her part – using both hands on the handle to unweight it from the ground and quickly nudge it forward using her whole body to heave and push at the same time.

While this was very cute and inspiring, it was a problem. Not only was this going to disrupt the process, but more importantly, I feared for her safety in the chaotic fury of people, shovels, buckets, and bags that were literally flying every which way. I had to get to her, but before I could signal my teammates and put down my current bucket of cement, I saw Jake power through a series of double-time shovel scoops, spear his shovel into the giant sand pile, and run over to the little girl. **Now, what he didn't do is the life-changing part. He didn't just take the bucket from her with a dismissive pat on the head to get her out of the way and keep the human assembly line rolling. He simply reached down, grabbed the handle right next to her hands and helped her take it to and dump it on the pile, gave her a high five, and went right back to the shoveling flurry.**

I am not sure anyone but me saw that happen – everyone was so busy and focused on the job at hand. But I am sure that Jake's 'small act of kindness' made a giant splash. That recognition of effort, helping hand for a shared mission, unspoken encouragement to contribute, and high-five tribute to her value and importance will no-doubt have a lasting impact on that tiny girl who wanted to help make a difference in the world. And, that tiny girl will no-doubt have a lasting impact on that community, which will no-doubt have a lasting impact on the world. That is a beautiful ripple effect that can be endless – if we all keep it going, one 'small act of kindness' at a time.

CHAPTER 3

GENEROSITY—Bob & Archie

No one has ever become poor by giving.

~Anne Frank

My Grandpa, Robert Gordon, was the main father figure in my life and one of the most amazing humans to walk the planet. And he would tell you that he married 'way over his head' with my Grandma, Frances – who he called Archie (he gave people who were close to him nicknames, which became a badge of honor for all who got one). Coming from a dirt-poor family who valued hard work, sharing whatever resources you had, and caring for others, he finished high school and took on three jobs to start his life with Archie and survive *The Great Depression*.

Even working three jobs and being a very engaged husband and father, he continued his education. Milk testing was a steady, good-paying job at the time, so he took a milk testing certification course and got the job. One of the other jobs he was able to get was sweeping the floors after hours at an international high tech manufacturing company. The company was integrally involved in making equipment for the war effort and Grandpa recognized that they needed more machinists. So, he asked to be a volunteer apprentice in order to earn a job that, by itself, could provide for his growing family. After earning that steady job as a machinist, he started devoting time to reading everything he could get his hands on about business, investing, and leadership; he joined a *Toastmasters* club and a *Rotary* club; he and Archie taught a Sunday School class together; and they volunteered for so many local service projects with the church, school, and community that everyone thought that there must be multiple Bob and Archie Gordons in their town because they were always "everywhere helping everyone."

My Grandma and Grandpa would be the first to tell you that they received far more than they gave, and that they did everything they did because they were trying to follow the Greatest Commandment:

You must love the Lord your God with all your heart, all your soul, all your strength, and all your mind. And, love your neighbor as yourself. (Luke 10:27, NLT)

...and that their greatest joy came in helping others. They both lived that out every single day of their lives. In fact, you would never know that Grandpa became president and CEO of that same international high tech manufacturing company that he swept the floors for, made millions of dollars through wise investments in the stock market, and gave millions of dollars to charitable organizations and educational institutions around the world. However, if you ever met him, you would know that he could never have done any of it without the love and support from Archie, and you would know that he automatically cared about you and would drop everything to help you however he could with whatever you needed. And, if you hung around long enough – you might even get a nickname – which was one of the many ways he would let you know that you were family to him, and he loved you.

In our first book, *Hand Delivered Hope*, I wrote about my favorite summer job of all time - being the crew for my Grandpa Gordon for when he would use his boat and gas to take all the kids and adults from the nearby lakefront homes waterskiing, tubing, and cruising pretty much non-stop throughout the summer. I would untangle ski ropes, adjust ski bindings, pick out the right life preserver, and relay the skiers' signals about boat speed, route, and duration to Captain Grandpa. Those cherished hours in the boat with him taught me his extremely strong work ethic, heart for others, giving spirit, unimpeachable character, and rock-solid faith.

Another thing about my grandparents that instilled core values in me that I am so grateful for was their true joy in giving. Since the earliest time I can remember, they would *always* pay for dinner for family and extended family, which included a lot of friends who were called family (and had nicknames). Being raised with good manners (under the 'penalty of death') and, quite honestly, thinking *wow, that is a lot of money,*

I would always go to him after every meal he paid for, hug him, and say, "Thank you, Grandpa! That was wonderful!"

He would always hold the hug for an extra moment, then look at me, smile the most authentic, caring smile, and say, "You are so very welcome, Jamie (my cherished nickname), I love you!"

When I got older and could afford to, I would say, "Grandpa, please let me pay for dinner, just one time!" And he would always just smile, and say, "Not this time."

Then, one time after he said that, I said, "Grandpa, why won't you let me or anyone else ever pay for dinner?"

He got very serious, put both of his hands on my shoulders and looked me dead in the eyes and said, ***"When you are the head of a family and you are able to, you always take care of that family, son! And, whenever you are not able to, you hold your head high and you ask that family for help. And, Jamie, remember, family is much, much more than blood. Do you understand me, son?"***

I said, "yes sir" and just gave him a hug – and held it for an extra moment.

Do you know the only time I ever got to pay for the family dinner? At his funeral.

So, when you are able to, take joy in the privilege of taking care of others. And, when you need others to take care of you, hold your head high, and allow them that privilege and joy. Not only is it the Greatest Commandment, it is one of the greatest ways to say, *I love you!*

Then, maybe give them a nickname. *Do you understand me?*

COMPASSION—Debbie

Compassion isn't about solutions. It's about giving all the love that you've got.

~Cheryl Strayed

I don't have a singular story to highlight compassion and that's the point – to me, compassion is a cultivated desire and capacity to constantly try to help others, and no one demonstrates that better for me than Debbie. In fact, it is such a part of who she is and how she lives her life that we have designated her as the CCO – Chief Compassion Officer – for our non-profit education-focused development aid organization. And, in case you are skeptically wondering, being our CCO is an unpaid, volunteer position.

In this world where the first response of many is often *What's in it for me?*, Debbie's response is always *Here's how I can help*. And, as I have learned and come to greatly appreciate, I want you to really soak in the subtle, but very important difference between *How can I help?* and **Here's how I can help.** The former puts the requirements for help back on the recipient. The person or people in-need then have to overcome the perceived and actual barriers to asking for help, decide if they deserve your help, determine what can and will help, figure out the associated logistics, and adjust their lives accordingly – all from within the eye of the storm. When we do the latter, we take on the requirements for help, truly coming to the aid of others to meet them in the storm, figure out what will help – an umbrella, a raincoat, a bucket, some boots, a warm towel, a hug – and then *do that* to the very best of our abilities and capacity.

That is compassion and that is what I have seen Debbie do time and time again. I have listened to her arrange transport for countless individuals who needed to get from point A to point B for medical care, educational and employment opportunities, family crises, or delivery of food, supplies, and resources. I have seen her facilitate driving lessons so that two men could get jobs to support their families. I have learned that she reserved and paid for a hotel room for a stranded family. I have heard her coordinate service trips for teachers, students, mechanics, contractors, doctors, nurses, and multilingual volunteers to make sure that key needs were met. I have watched her give her last bottle of water, serving of food, rain poncho, pair of gloves, hat, and dollar to 'someone who needed it more.' And, I have personally felt her warm embrace many times when I was in the storms of sorrow, frustration, hurt, and grief.

What a beautiful gift it is to receive compassion – to have someone come to you in the storm and say *Here's how I can help.* It is life-giving to know that someone sees you, hears you, and cares – cares enough to meet you where you are, take on the requirements of helping, and walk beside you through the storm. Like the quote at the start of this chapter, Debbie has taught me that it is not about solving someone's problems for them, it is about being there to help by giving them all of the love that you've got.

CHAPTER 5

HUMILITY—Glenn

True humility is staying teachable regardless of how much you already know.

~Anonymous

One of the most striking examples of true humility that I have ever seen is my friend Glenn. I met Glenn in Butare, Rwanda where we were both involved in a school renovation service project. Glenn was seventy-eight years young at the time. Standing all of 5'6" tall and rail thin, Glenn is a giant – with his wife, Genie (whom he gives all the credit to for everything), he raised eleven amazing kids and built an extremely successful life by all the usual measures, starting from nothing as a door-to-door salesman to become a corporate and community leader, real estate magnate, and extraordinary philanthropist. But what makes Glenn a giant to me is his humility.

The first time I remember seeing Glenn, he was sitting in a plastic chair on the small porch of a Rwandan guesthouse room dressed in lace-up work boots, mismatched athletic socks, worn and paint-splotched corduroy shorts, a threadbare faded-logo T-shirt, and a tattered *Habitat for Humanity* hat. Add a pair of wrap-around sunglasses, multiple band-aids and bruises, and at least two African, Indian, Papua New Guinean, or Peruvian children at his side, and that is how I will always see Glenn in my mind's eye. That is Glenn, inside and out – authentic, no pretense, no hubris, no assumptions – 'just a normal guy' who takes an all-in others-first approach to everything he does. He wants to get to know you, learn from you, and work with you to make your world, and our world, better.

I have seen Glenn model this humility in at least nine countries, and although it comes in the form of different methods and mechanisms, the motives and the impacts reverberate in the same incredible ways. Time after time, year after year, Glenn gives his time, talents, and treasures to travel from Columbus, Ohio to the other side of the world to humbly serve others.

By day, he dons his 'project uniform,' pulls those sunglasses down like a gladiator sets his face shield as he steps into the arena, and gets to work. And man, does he ever work...hard! I have seen him clear brush, dig ditches, haul bricks, carry lumber, shovel gravel, hand-mix cement, saw boards, pound nails, raise walls, push wheelbarrows, assemble desks, set doors, paint classrooms, and varnish floors - all day, every day, with the best of them. He will do the odd jobs, dirty jobs, grueling jobs, boring jobs, and scary jobs. He will work ahead of you, behind you, or by your side. He will work with men, women, boys, and girls, who speak his language or do not speak his language.

By night, he plays 'crazy faces,' football, and slap hands with the local kids until *they* get tired, then asks them about school, their families, and their dreams, and then tells them a story or two – always with a lesson or a message. Then, he cleans up and dresses up for dinner where he always sits with a different person each night so he can hear their stories and learn something new. Whenever I ask him about the new person he met, he always starts with "Jimi, I just think she (or he) is great!" and then gives me specifics as to why, what he learned, and how he will apply it to his life. After dinner, he takes his dishes to the kitchen and thanks and compliments the chefs. Then, he engages in whatever the evening activities are, including more conversation, dancing, card playing, games, or music – until *everyone else* gets tired and goes to bed.

And, in between international mission projects, I am not sure what he wears, but it should include a cape because he thinks about, dreams up, plans, and strategizes ways to provide facilities, resources, funding, and opportunities for people all over the world who he has never met (yet) to improve their education, health, and lives.

Yep, he is a superhero, but **you would never know it unless you saw how he unassumingly uses his superpowers to help others – and even then, he would make sure that you walked away feeling like the superhero and that it was his honor and privilege to get to know you.**

One of the many great examples of this and one of my most treasured memories is about 'the bridge that Glenn built.' On one of our school-building projects in a little village in Peru, Glenn saw a problem that he really wanted to fix. The quarter-mile trek from the village to the school was a pretty tough and treacherous narrow jungle path. While the students and teachers could paddle their canoes back to the school during the rainy season and could carefully walk all the way to the school in the dry season, the many months between the two seasons left the path as a swampy, muddy, snake-infested mess. So, near the end of the project, Glenn came to me and said, "Jimi, we have to do something about that walk to school for these kids. It's not safe. Can we build a bridge? If BTCV and the community can build it, the Willett Family (his family) will fund it." I told him that I wasn't sure, but that we would get to work on it.

One year later, Glenn made another splash in the world as he pounded the last nail on the decking for a quarter-mile long bridge over that path. The Willett Family Bridge is above flood stage and safely connects the village to the school in all seasons. To me, it is the most beautiful bridge the world has ever seen, because it is a bridge to the future—each child that walks on the bridge from the village to the school to get an education is walking toward their goals, their dreams, and their futures. Fittingly, the last and lasting image I have from that project is Glenn standing on that bridge in lace-up work boots, mismatched athletic socks, worn and paint-splotched corduroy shorts, a threadbare faded-logo T-shirt, a tattered hat, and a pair of wrap-around sunglasses with multiple band-aids and bruises all over him, holding the hands of three beautiful Peruvian children who were getting ready to walk toward their better futures thanks to a humble man named Glenn – authentic, no pretense, no hubris, no assumptions – 'just a normal guy' who is making the world a better place, one splash at a time.

Portions of this chapter were adapted from, *Hand Delivered Hope*, Trilogy 2020

CHAPTER 6

GRIT—Ethan

I can be changed by what happens to me, but I refuse to be reduced by it.

~Maya Angelou

The voice on the phone had a strong Boston accent.

"Dr. Cook, this is Ethan, we have been communicating by email about a research position in your lab. I am excited about the in-person interview, thank you, but I do need to tell you before our meeting that I'm in a chair."

"You're in a chair?"

"Yeah...sorry, a wheelchair. I have CP...cerebral palsy...and I'm in a chair, a wheelchair...pretty much full time."

"Ah, got it. Thanks for letting me know. The lab is on the second floor, so take the elevator to the right when you come in the building, okay? See you tomorrow, right?"

"Uh, yeah, okay then Dr. Cook. See you then, then – tomorrow, I mean – yeah, tomorrow is then, so I will see you then. Thank you."

I did not realize until later – much later – that Ethan thought that phone call would likely change things regarding him working with me. Well, he was right, it actually changed everything.

The next day, I met Ethan by the second-floor elevators, took him on a tour of the lab, and hired him on the spot. Just like the call he made the previous day, he was so honest about everything – never using anything as an excuse, but pragmatically communicating challenges and addressing questions, that we had and he had, in a manner that not only put us all at ease but helped us learn and gain perspective. Ethan quickly became a valued member of the lab, and he and I became fast friends. We talked about sports, adaptive sports, his family, his classes, and education. He confided in me that he was not all that interested in orthopaedic research, but really needed a job with flexible hours and he heard from a friend that our lab allowed that. He told me that his dream was to be a teacher and a comedian ("but don't call it stand-up comedy, Dr. Cook, get it?!"). I told him about our school-building organization+ and suggested that he go on a project with us.

"Are you being for real, Dr. Cook?"

"Of course I am, Ethan, that would be great!"

"Okay, yeah, maybe, yeah maybe I could...we'll see...but until then, how do I get involved now?"

I smiled a knowing smile. I could tell he was hooked, and this was going to happen and that it was going to be life-changing – at least for me.

Ethan became BTCV's first *Intern for Change* and helped us with our website, fundraising, and project planning. He also helped us set up a site evaluation for a new project in Guatemala City. He was really engaged and interested in that process and so when we were finalizing the plans for it, I said, "Ethan, why don't you go with us? You know this proposal better than anyone now, and I could sure use your help. Then, you can do your first BTCV build too since we will join the team in Chichi after the evaluation is completed."

"For real?"

"For real!"

We talked to Ethan's parents together, got their approval, coordinated schedules, made all the travel plans, and made the trip from Columbia, MO to meet Glenn at the airport in Guatemala City. On the trip from the US, where physical disabilities are largely accommodated, I still got a first-hand education on the physical, psychological, and emotional hurdles and barriers that exist and are created by able-bodied people like me.

I watched, and sometimes helped, Ethan navigate hauling his luggage, getting in and out of the car, bathroom stalls and sinks, store aisles and counters, and curbs with determination and grace. I watched him notice the stares from kids, and adults, and return them all with a genuine smile. I watched people be unsure of what to do, ignore him, cut in front of him, and dismiss him while he tolerated it with heart-breaking familiarity and inspiring patience and resilience. I was starting to learn what real grit is all about.

Then, we visited the small non-profit center housed next to the infamous Guatemala City Dump.* This incredible organization was providing healthcare, hygiene training, nourishment, and after-school support and education to families who lived in the shanty towns within the dump. They welcomed us and then said that the first order of business was for us to tour the giant landfill in order for us to see how the more than 13,000 inhabitants, more than half of whom are kids, scratched out an existence, and understand, first-hand, their challenges, hurdles, and needs.

For all of us, the tour was a surreal scene that was immensely emotionally challenging. First, the smell was overwhelming and not something we 'got used to' at any level. Then, the sites were almost indescribable – in the center of the forty-plus acres of endless trash, there were literally thousands of people, young and old, climbing over garbage mountains, following giant earth-mover machines, sorting through the 'good stuff,' and hauling away everything you have ever seen 'put out in the trash' by the rich and the poor, and many things you haven't seen from either. They take their daily finds to the shanty towns which surround the periphery of the landfill to sort, clean, repair, and refurbish them to use, sell, or trade. Their dwellings are tiny patchwork structures pieced together from scraps of 'pre-owned' cardboard, plastic, wood, metal, milk crates, egg cartons, billboards, road signs, tires, car parts, and shingles. The shanty towns are tight-packed with narrow, semi-cleared alleys that rival game-show obstacle courses because of the people, merchandise, work benches, and sorting stacks that jut in and out and up and down from seemingly every direction. It is sensory overload in the most intense and despairing sense of the words.

For Ethan, it was also physically challenging. Imagine navigating all of that in a wheelchair. I'll be honest, I don't think I could have done it. But Ethan did. He told us that if he was going to be part of the assessment and decision-making process, then he needed to see, feel, hear, and experience everything first-hand. He needed to understand what the inhabitants were going through and what they saw as the needs, barriers, and best ways to create sustainable solutions. So, he made it through the narrow alleys, over the drainage ditches, around the obstacles of every type – allowing Glenn and me to give him a push or a pull when needed – and into the cramped quarters of the homes we visited to meet kids, parents, and grandparents that the organization was serving. Ethan asked questions, took notes, snapped pictures (after asking), and listened intently.

The three of us discussed our perceptions, emotions, findings, and ideas for this project on the long van ride from Guatemala City to Chichicastenango (Chichi). It was definitely a somber discussion, but it was also full of hope because of the people working in the mission and the grit and determination from dump inhabitants that we met. They did not feel sorry for themselves and definitely did not want you to feel sorry for them. They were grateful for help when it came in the form of opportunity. And ***Ethan's presence and perspective highlighted this 'empathy not sympathy' and 'opportunity not charity' approach that has been one of the most important perspective shifts I have ever had.***

This was further accentuated in Chichi, when we visited some of the families who were walking miles and miles each day for their children to receive educational opportunities. The small shacks that the families lived in were built on a very steep, very rugged, and even treacherous hill in this beautiful area of the world. This presented a bit of a problem for the planned home visit. We had some older individuals with us on this project and Ethan was in his wheelchair. We surveyed the scene. The older volunteers and Ethan did not want to hold up the group or inconvenience anyone and so they immediately offered to wait in the van. This did not sit right with me, so I blurted out, "No, we came here as a team to visit these amazing families and we are going to do this as team. Let's form a chain, go slow, and get down to those homes together, okay?" Like a close-knit football team breaking the huddle for a critical play to win the game, the whole team immediately answered, "let's do it!" and so we got organized, linked up like a ragamuffin congo line and started our way down the steep hill to the two homes we were to visit. Ethan can walk with assistance, if two people – one in front and one behind – steady him and help him swing his legs as he goes. So, we started very slowly and carefully and then picked up the pace a bit as we all got our rhythm on the descent. It took quite a while, but there were no falls, no injuries, and no quitters. Quite the opposite, in fact, there was lots of laughing, communicating, encouraging, and cheering. And, our 'big play' worked, we made it down to the two homes, did a round of high-fives, wiped the sweat off our brows, and were filled with joy as we imbibed the wonderful welcoming smiles that the families had waiting for us as they received us into their homes.

Similar to the Guatemala City shanty towns, the homes were makeshift wooden structures that appeared to be cobbled together from whatever materials the families could find and fashion into a shelter. As we always experience with these beautiful souls who have almost nothing in a material sense, they offered us everything they did have. We had tea and bread. We sat on benches, logs, and the floor and had wonderful conversations (through interpreters) about their childhoods, marriages, families, dreams, children, and dreams for their children. We saw their small gardens and crops. Ethan asked questions, took notes, snapped pictures (after asking), and listened intently. We all listened intently, and so we learned, we felt, we understood, we empathized. Hope burned bright in that gathering of people from very different worlds, different languages, different resources, and different ways of life – and that hope filled us all up, uniting us to share a common spirit of humanity and humanness that is spreading ripples around the world to this day.

The trek up the hill was even harder and more treacherous. I put Ethan on my back and used a very awkward and comical all-fours climbing technique with some verbal and physical encouragement from the team to make it back to the top. However, when we got to the top, we had way *more* energy than we did before we even took one step down the hill. The resilience, strength, and purpose of this amazing community filled our tanks to overflowing, and it was an experience that none of us will ever forget.

The project in Chichi was to build a playground for kids with special needs. Not only did Ethan do the work of at least three people on this project – digging, shoveling, mixing, hauling, constructing, assembling, painting - but he was also able to design, set up, and test the playground equipment so that it would *really work* for kids with different types of special needs. He paid attention to every detail to make sure everything was safe, accessible, and feasible for the kids, their teachers, and caregivers. I do think he tested each swing a couple extra times to make really, really sure they were good – and the huge smile on his face as he swung joyfully on each of them made me certain that this playground would have generational impact.

Ethan's next school-building project with BTCV was in Malawi. Not only did his parents allow him to go on this trip – they came with him! *And guess who Ethan worked with during that project?* Sam! It was so amazing to see these two interact, work together – and yep, play soccer together! Two incredible young men who had been struck with physical disabilities that they overcame to change their lives and the world. I cannot think of two more determined, grittier people who inspire me each and every day and who I am so proud to call two of my dearest friends in the world.

Ethan has gone on to complete a graduate degree and is now teaching – and doing live comedy – inspiring people to face their challenges, overcome them, and then help others to do the same, creating ripples of grit and determination that are changing the world.

Portions of this chapter were adapted from, *Hand Delivered Hope*, Trilogy 2020
+*Be The Change Volunteers* (BTCV) is a US-based development aid non-profit organization dedicated to creating better education opportunities worldwide. http://www.bethechangevolunteers.org
* https://www.youtube.com/watch?v=7Jwo-otMKxY

CHAPTER 7

COURAGE—Dolly

I learned that courage was not the absence of fear, but the triumph over it.

~Nelson Mandela

Dolly is a beautiful Peruvian woman who stands all of five feet tall at best and is very petite, but there is more courage packed into that tiny frame than I have seen in any other human I know. Add to her small size that she literally lives and works in the heart of the very rugged and austere Amazon Jungle, as a woman, in a very strongly patriarchal culture, and you might expect her to be very careful to 'not make waves'. But I have seen her stand up to government officials, village ladies' inebriated husbands, crooked businessmen, overbearing philanthropists, lazy community members, out-of-line employees, and unruly students. I have watched her boldly advocate for education, healthcare, women's rights, and social justice. I have witnessed her build and lead a non-profit organization, an ecotourism business, an artisan's co-op, and more development aid projects than I can count. And, I have heard her tell how she felt each and every time that she stepped into these situations, processes, and projects.

"I was terrified!" she said, "But, I knew in each situation that there was something bigger at stake, something more important, that allowed me to overcome my fear and keep talking, working, trying...and just...doing...to try to get the result we wanted."

When I asked her where that comes from, she immediately replied, "From my family." In different ways, her grandmother, mother, and father all instilled in her this strong capacity to face her fears and keep going.

Importantly, they all made certain that the "bigger, more important purpose" was identified first and that it was determined to be noble and good. They raised her to believe that her female sex, size, status, and position should not define her or limit her. They modeled a strong work ethic, the value of education, appreciation for what you have, empathy for others, seizing opportunities, passion, and perseverance in all that they did. Dolly certainly paid attention to these role models and incorporated their values into her life very well, using each and every one of these ingrained traits to help others and make the world a better place.

I got to see this in full effect and let it wash over me again on a recent trip to Peru for another one of our school-building projects in El Chino. The volunteer team just sat down in the Maloca – the open-walled thatched-roof rotunda that is the center of village life – to be welcomed, make introductions, get an orientation, hear the plans, and receive assignments before getting to work. We traveled to the village that morning on the Tahuayo tributary of the Amazon River using one of Dolly's boats, coming from the internationally heralded one-of-a-kind ecotourism lodge that Dolly and her husband, Paul, built and run. On the fifteen-minute river cruise, Dolly enthusiastically pointed out the incredible Amazonian flora and fauna, called out to the local inhabitants that were starting their morning activities along the banks and in hand-hewn canoes, and made sure that each team member was feeling okay and ready for an adventure.

After arriving in the village, Dolly was sitting next to me on a bench in the Maloca, and while everyone was getting organized and the Peruvian band was tuning up to play, she brought me up to speed on the daily schedule, the supplies and equipment deliveries, the community's work assignments, the principal's availability, the teachers' workshops in Iquitos, the expert she brought in from Lima to evaluate our plans for solar energy on campus, the new community members, the status and funding for students from Chino who had gone on to university, vocational training, and jobs, and the accommodations she had arranged for a team member who had an injury right before leaving the US. In between and during each of these itemized reports, one of the Chino kids would come up to Dolly to give her a hug.

Trying not to interrupt her conversation with the 'big American' too much, they would start to jet back to where they were talking or playing with friends, but Dolly would grab each one by the hand, the shirt, or sometimes the ear – and during a quick break in our conversation - ask them about school. Each one would dutifully give 'Ms. Dolly' their report and if it was not detailed enough, or she sensed some concealing of information, she would hold the hand, shirt, or ear a bit longer until she got the whole truth. Then, she would praise and encourage them, let them go, and continue the cycle until she and I were fully updated on our respective reports.

Now, it was time for the ceremony. The Peruvian military regional commander, mayor, school board chairman, band leader, co-op president, and contractor were all shooting anxious but deferential looks of *we're ready* at Dolly. As she patted me on the knee twice, Dolly stood up to her full height and walked to the center of the Maloca in her camouflage T-shirt, cargo capri pants, and gum boots. Each of these other individuals towered over her in height, but none did in 'presence.' She graciously acknowledged the entire crowd, in Spanish and English, celebrated the purpose for this occasion and extolled BTCV and the community for partnering together on this full campus project, and reminded us all about the value and power of education throughout our lives.

Then, with the military commander standing right next to her in full regalia and oozing bravado in anticipation of his time in the spotlight, she went on to say, "We want to welcome and thank our esteemed leaders for joining us in this joyous and profound ceremony, and we will hear from each of these men. But first, I want to have our mayor (the first woman to be mayor of Chino, who Dolly advocated and campaigned for) share her vision for this project, this school, and this community."

 The mayor spoke. Each of the men, including me, spoke. Then, Dolly wrapped it up with passion and purpose, let the band get through three songs, motioned to the team, picked up a bag of supplies for the first day's work, and led us back to the job site to get to work.

This was just another one of the many situations in Dolly's life when there was something bigger and more important at stake – value and respect for women as community leaders – and just another one of the many times that she overcame her fear and kept talking, working, trying...and just...doing...to try to get the result we wanted...and needed.

Does it surprise you at all that we call her the 'Peruvian Wonder Woman?' She may not fit the physical stereotype of that Marvel Comics Superhero, but she sure does fit, and actually exceed, her strength and courage to help and inspire others by facing her fears and making waves of hope that change the world.

CHAPTER 8

GRATITUDE—Bartalomeo

Gratitude makes sense of our past, brings peace for today, and creates a vision for tomorrow.
~Melody Beattie

Do you know what your chances of survival are if you are born with a disability in rural Guatemala? While I cannot provide accurate statistics, let me put it this way. In Chichicastenango, and many villages like it, there is a hill set aside for the sole purpose of throwing babies with disabilities over it as soon as the problem is recognized. While this seems calloused and maybe even evil to you and me, it is driven by both reality and religion, and it is deeply ingrained in the culture. The religious aspect is that disabilities are viewed as a curse or an evil spirit. The reality aspect is that theirs is a life of survival. Feeding your family is hard, and if one of the mouths you are feeding is not attached to a body or mind that can eventually contribute to family survival in the traditional ways as they grow up, then 'survival of the fittest' comes into play for them.

Bartalomeo did not subscribe to 'the hill approach' and instead he looked for a way to allow his severely disabled daughter, Joselin, to not only survive, but to thrive. Fighting enormous societal, and often family pressures, and pushing against overwhelming financial odds, Bartalomeo dedicated extraordinary amounts of time and energy to care for Joselin's special needs. He adapted her bed, chair, bathtub, and toilet and would cook special food for her and feed her himself to make sure she got enough nutrition. Bartalomeo also fashioned a cart of sorts from an old vendor wagon so that he could pull Joselin several miles each way, each day to one of the very few resources for kids with special needs, and their families, at a wonderful Christian mission center in the hills of Chichi. This organization provides education, nutrition, and physical therapy to kids with special needs whose families said no to 'the hill.'

Our school-building organization had partnered with this mission to complete two beautiful classrooms designed for students with special needs – and their families. And, a really special component was that the kids and the families definitely did their part – including Bartalomeo and Joselin. They carried supplies, painted walls, and assembled school chairs, desks, and equipment. And the difference these classrooms made to the students, teachers, and families – physically and emotionally – was more than can be described in words. These classrooms provided a true learning environment and allowed for more educational activities and more individual attention for meeting the needs of each student. Most importantly, it validated the hard work these families did to avoid 'the hill' - it said, *your children are valuable, they deserve a quality education, and they can contribute.*

So, we decided to go back to Chichi to help build a playground at this center. Now, you might be asking yourself, *A playground?! For kids with special needs? In the developing world? Wouldn't there be much better use of time and funds for them? Couldn't you do something better for them?*

Well, *did you know that kids, especially in the developing world, do significantly better in their studies and placement examinations when the school day includes dedicated time for recreation and sport? Did you know that physical education at school improves child health, increases attendance, and heightens social and employment skills? Did you learn from Sam and Ethan that opportunity for inclusion in all aspects of school and life is a key element in a child's development, education, and sense of self-worth?*

The final push for this project came from what we observed during our first project in Chichi. The current playground for the center was right near the entrance to the whole complex. So, the kids with special needs would go past that playground each day on the way to their classrooms. They would see all the other kids playing on swings, jungle gym, teeter totter, and merry-go-round. The kids on the playground always seemed to be having so much fun and getting so much joy from the experience. They were laughing, joking, smiling, and squealing with delight as the kids with special needs would get pushed or carried past the scene each day.

So, we were convinced that a special needs playground was actually the very best thing we could do at this school, and we took Ethan with us back to Chichi and worked with the kids, parents, and teachers to help them build a playground and garden area that the kids with special needs and their families could find joy in too. At the dedication and celebration ceremony for the completed special needs playground, Bartalomeo gave a barely audible speech, with his head down and tears dripping onto the front of his embroidered cha-queta. His words did not leave a dry eye in the house. He told us all that the only words he could think of to try to describe his overwhelming emotions were *xumaltioxij ri toq' ob ri xban che* ("so very grateful" in K'iche'). He said that he could never discard her and that he will never discard his feelings for us and what we did to make them both feel whole.

We think it was a great decision and a fantastic result, but we will let you decide for yourself. After returning home, we received the following message in an email from our project partner in Chichi.

Subject: First time on a swing – PURE JOY!!

> *Dear BTCV,*
>
> *This morning in the mountains of Guatemala, I found 11-year-old, Joselin, sitting in her wheelchair happily tugging on one of the swings in the "normal kids" playground.*
>
> *While watching her, I realized that this little girl was probably imagining what it would be like to swing, but her twisted body had never experienced that before.*
>
> *We talked with her father, Bartalomeo, and he pushed her down the sidewalk to the BTCV Special Needs Playground - we had just the thing for little Joselin. As we opened the wheelchair swing and put the ramp down, her dad pushed her onto the first swing she'd ever been on. Once she was secure, the fun began. Joselin's face was bright with a beautiful smile as she soared in the breeze of her first swing ride.*

On that swing, she was "normal," she was "whole," she was filled with the pure joy that every kid needs and deserves.

Thank you for helping make this possible!

Attached were pictures of Joselin on that swing, with the biggest smile on her face you have ever seen – you could see the pure joy oozing from her whole body. And you could see the same from her father, Bartalomeo, in the background. A father who chose to go against every cultural, religious, societal, familial, and financial pressure to say no to 'the hill' and give Joselin a life filled with education, experiences, love and joy! **Let that wash over you and fill you with gratitude.**

Portions of this chapter were adapted from, *Hand Delivered Hope*, Trilogy 2020

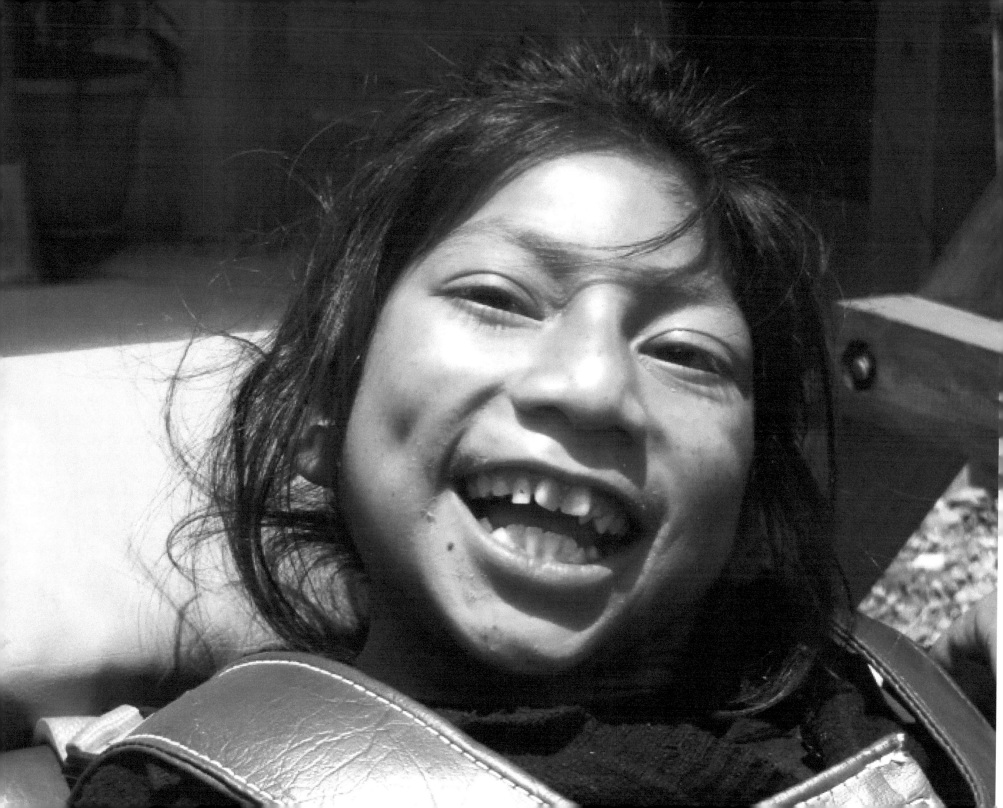

CHAPTER 9

EMPATHY—Reachana

The nature of humanity, its essence, is to feel another's pain as one's own, and to act to take that pain away. There is nobility in compassion, a beauty in empathy, a grace in forgiveness.

~John Connolly

My friend, John, and I were standing on the awning-covered walkway outside of baggage claim at Siem Reap International Airport waiting for whomever was supposed to pick us up. We were pretty sure that someone was going to show up, but we weren't totally sure who it would be as that detail was a bit 'lost in communication' over the past few months as we planned this trip to Cambodia. We weren't at all worried, just a bit jet-lagged from the long trip and the time change and wondering whether our transport would be in the form of a van, tuk-tuk, motorcycle, or other vehicle, and if we should be looking for a sign with our names on it or some other way to find our driver.

Quite a few of all types of the aforementioned vehicles showed up, picked up passengers, and headed out to their various destinations. It was still crowded and busy with human and vehicular traffic when I heard a small but very enthusiastic voice repeating with ever-increasing volume, "Daddy! Daddy! I see you, Daddy!" and noticed the biggest smile come over John's face as I turned toward the sound of the voice, saw a small figure emerge from the crowd, and was immediately embraced by the warmest and most wonderful hug. It was Reachana - she found a way to come get us herself so that we could reunite as soon as possible.

I met Reachana nine years prior to this trip, when our school-building organization built a Floating Learning Center for a large Vietnamese community living on Tonle Sap Lake near Siem Reap, Cambodia. Our meeting was truly miraculous in many ways. Reachana literally showed up out of nowhere like an angel sent from heaven right when we needed her most. We were in the midst of trying to help a young boy with a broken arm who had been very ineffectually treated by a local witch doctor and was at risk for having a very crooked, painful, non-functional dominant arm for the rest of his life. Unfortunately, his Vietnamese parents were not interested in our help if it involved western medicine and neither my southern-accented English nor our Cambodian guides' Khmer were having any convincing effects on them. Finally, using a bit of charades, and I think based on the pained and distraught look on their son's face, they allowed us to look at it. But, only under the very watchful eyes of the family, and a rapidly growing crowd of onlookers who wondered what 'black magic' we were going to perform.

Cristi, my wife, and I sat down with the injured boy, Uk, on a bench and were completely surrounded by onlookers. I started gently cleaning the wound on Uk's broken and crooked arm. I was working through a process of scrubbing, straightening, looking up and smiling, scrubbing, straightening, looking up and smiling, when all of a sudden there was another set of hands scrubbing his arm – pretty vigorously I must say. I looked up to see what was going on and saw the face of a young girl sitting right next to me. I had no idea who she was, how she got there, and why she was trying to help (so vigorously) and did not know how I was going to deal with this new variable. So, in my best loud voice (because that always helps people interpret your language) with my best charades, I said and demonstrated, "CAREFUL! BROKEN! ARM HURT! GENTLE!" In perfect English, she said, "I know, I am here to help you."

It was not the time to ask for details from her, so I simply said, "Okay, thanks," and we got back to work. She held his arm, helped clean, and explained everything to the parents and onlookers in what I learned later was perfect Vietnamese and perfect Khmer. Together, we got Uk's arm cleaned up, fixed up, and properly bandaged. As soon as we did, all the color came back to his face and he gave us a big smile. All was good, especially after Reachana translated our advice for getting a cast put on the arm as soon as possible and how that would "make his arm come right" so he could go back to doing all the things a thirteen-year-old Vietnamese boy should do.

When the dust settled and the crowd cleared, I said, "Reachana, thank you for your help – you did a great job, and I am very grateful! How did you learn to speak three languages so well?" She said simply, "School."

We learned about her love for learning, her against-all-odds determination to keep going to school no matter what, learning three languages and scoring high enough on the national exam to follow her dream – "a proper university education and degree." When we learned that the only thing preventing her from pursuing her dream was funding, it was a no-brainer to provide the support that she needed. We got Reachana all set up with funding for school and the only 'return on investment' we asked for was for her to keep us updated on her progress and use her education and training to help her community in some way in the future.

Throughout her schooling, we received regular emails and irregular phone calls - always between 2 and 3 a.m. our time as she could never quite figure out the time difference – but we were used to dead-of-night phone calls since as veterinarians, we both took overnight call, and Reachana always began the calls with, "Daddy (or Mommy), is that you?" With that term of endearment and respect starting a call from an amazing young lady who was fighting all odds to learn, mature, and accomplish her big hairy audacious goal (BHAG) for her family and community, *how could we ever be the least bit upset?* And we never were.

Reachana fulfilled all her promises and more. She followed up on Uk and made sure he got proper care. About two months after we got home from Cambodia, we received an email from her saying, *Uk's arm is fine. Cast removed and arm very straight. He and family happy,* with a picture attached – of her standing next to Uk on the Floating Learning Center. Both of his arms were extended in front of him to show how straight his fractured arm had healed and how well the wound had mended as well.

Both of them had beautiful big smiles on their faces.

She completed her schooling and did go back to the floating village to support their passion for education. A beautiful testament of this was a picture from a site visit sent to us of Reachana, sitting cross-legged on the floor of the Floating Learning Center, next to a tiny Vietnamese girl of about four or five years old. Reachana is tending to a small scrape on the little girl's arm. The little girl is sitting cross-legged too in her beautiful school uniform looking up at Reachana with an unmistakable look of awe-inspired hero-worship. The look says it all – *Reachana did it, now I know I can too!*

And, back to our visit nine years later, Reachana lives and works in Siem Reap and now has a beautiful family of her own, including her husband and two daughters and another child on the way. In addition to her full-time job and busy life as a very engaged mom, she regularly visits the Floating Learning Center, bringing supplies, working with them on nutrition, hygiene, and healthcare, and encouraging them to continue their educations in pursuit of their own dreams.

She was an incredible host for our visit, taking us to the Floating Learning Center and other schools in the area, lining up interviews with community partners, school administrators, teachers, parents, and students, planning for subsequent projects, and teaching us more about the educational system, politics, and culture in Cambodia. The most impactful and inspiring part of the visit though was when Reachana introduced us to three children from her village and had them tell us about their lives, education, and dreams. They each relayed beautiful stories filled with hope and passion about loving to go to school, getting to go to the 'best' schools, and following their dreams. We had also learned that each had few if any living family members, little if any family income, and no means for school tuition, uniforms, books, supplies, or transportation. When we asked how they were able to go to the 'best' schools and do so well, they all had the same two-word answer, "Ms. Reachana!" When we asked Reachana why she decided to help these children when she has her own kids to support with very limited resources, she said, ***"Because we should not only see the world through our own eyes!"*** Reachana knew their struggles, dreamed their dreams, felt their pain, and lived their search for hope. So, she decided to act to take away their pain, to walk with them through the storm, to give them the hope that she had found - she made a splash in their lives. That is the beauty – and the ripple effect - of empathy.

Let that wash over you...again and again and again...

Portions of this chapter were adapted from, *Hand Delivered Hope*, Trilogy 2020

CHAPTER 10

JOY—Phomotso

Joy is a net of love by which you can catch souls.

~Mother Teresa

"He said that you need to talk to the sheep", Thato said in his deep, soothing South African accent as he looked at me with concern and compassion.

We were standing in the shared open ground of the village where Phomotso, our adopted South African son, was born and raised, looking out toward the beautiful Eastern Cape vista where we had just finished the graveside memorial service for him.

The emotions were deep and complex, and the gravity of seeing Phomotso laid to rest in the tiny village that he came so far from to accomplish all his big hairy audacious goals (BHAGs) was overwhelming.

Thato - Phomotso's college roommate and best friend, who traveled all the way from Pretoria to be with us – was the only one fluent in both English and Sesotho and so he had to translate everything that the village elders said to us. This last one, translated to me, as Cristi and I stood less than six feet away from the family's most valuable lamb who was being held by the village's official 'end of life team,' was a bit confusing to say the least. At first, I did wonder if something got lost in translation for this one, so I politely and respectfully probed a bit more in a quiet 'sidebar' with Thato.

"So, I need to actually speak to the sheep at this point?"

"Yes"

"Out loud?"

"Yes"

"Is there something specific that I should say?"

"Whatever is in your heart at this moment."

A bunch of other questions including, *Should I speak in English? Should I kneel down so I am at sheep-level? and Should I ask the sheep for its last words?* were also on my mind, but when Thato said, "whatever is in your heart," all the swirling thoughts and questions came into a streamlined focus that took me back to a phone call I had with Phomotso the week before his graduation ceremony. With his voice shaking with the combination of disbelief, excitement, accomplishment, and pure joy, he said to me, "We did it, Dad!"

That was one of the many, many things that Phomotso taught me – true and pure joy! And he did that so many times in so many ways - from the first time he told me he wanted to be a photojournalist to the first time he got to take pictures with a real camera to his coming to live with us and go to school in the US - and so many more. I think it is so important to differentiate being happy, feeling good, and having fun from *pure joy*, and Phomotso helped me learn that.

And he exuded that joy every day to everyone around him. As a testament to that, at a small memorial we held at his American high school, where schoolmate after schoolmate from 2nd grade to alumni told their 'Phomotso stories,' each one either started or ended by saying, *and I was his best friend!* And none of them were lying. Phomotso legitimately had so many best friends and treated them all that way. His smile lit up every room he entered, and when he was with you, he was present – fiercely present. **When he talked with you, all of the other sounds and noises became silent, and you entered into connection that was palpable and profound. You could see and feel him absorbing your thoughts and emotions, allowing them to resonate deep in his very soul, and ignite a spark that returned the light of joy back to both of you.** When you asked him what the best part of a play, movie, trip, or adventure was, he would always authentically say, *Everything!* When you asked him why he ate his salad last, why he liked country music, or why he loved holding babies and talking with senior citizens, he would always lovingly say, *Because it makes my soul smile!* And, when you asked him why photojournalism brought him so much joy, he would always thoughtfully say, *Because one picture can tell a person's entire story and I want to tell people's stories!*

This amazing young man from a no-name village in South Africa completed his degree in photojournalism - his BHAG-come-true - and I was all set to see him graduate. I was booked to fly to South Africa early on a Saturday morning when I received a call from Thato Friday evening telling me that Phomotso had just passed away. Three days before his graduation ceremony, an undiagnosed, asymptomatic heart condition caused sudden death in his sleep. We were in shock. Devastated. Lost. Broken. And, while we are still broken hearted, we know that he accomplished his dream and brought joy to so many lives along the way and these ripples of joy have turned into waves of love and hope that are washing over hearts all around the world... again and again and again.

So, I did kneel down to sheep-level, and I did speak in English:

Thank you for letting us honor our son, Phomotso, in this traditional way in this village where he was born, where he dreamed big dreams as a little boy, where he learned the power of hope, the strength of empathy, and the beauty of true joy. He taught us so much about life and love. Our South African son was a true Changer who left a legacy of passion, positivity, and joy that will never be forgotten.* Because of him, we learned how to be parents, we learned that true family has little to do with genetics and nearly everything to do with sharing life together, and we learned that miracles really do happen and that a simple conversation, a willing heart, and one person who cares and says "Here's how I can help" can start a ripple effect that can change the world. He was the greatest ever at telling a person's story with a single picture, and I am so glad that I got to be his best friend! And I will end by telling you the best thing about him – everything!

---

* I hope that you will take the time to read his story and see some of his work on our website http://www.bethechangevolunteers.org/phomotsos-page.html.

CHAPTER 11

FORGIVENESS—Beata

Forgiveness does not change the past, but it does enlarge the future.

~Paul Boose

"No, I don't believe you", Beata replied just a few short but seemingly eternal seconds after answering the telephone. Her sister-in-law had called to painfully stammer out the overwhelming news that Beata's husband and father-in-law had been killed by the Interahamwe militia in Butare. Even though the Rwandan civil war and subsequent genocide had been a source of daily fear and worry for four years, and they had witnessed many horrific atrocities first-hand, it still was something that she couldn't – and shouldn't have had to – believe. The two men had gone out together to just run a quick errand. But, on their way home they were stopped by a militia group, forcibly walked several miles to an isolated area outside the city and mutilated and dismembered before being killed and thrown into a pit. They were not doing anything wrong, they were unarmed, and they did not incite any violence. They were in the wrong place at the wrong time in the middle of an unfathomable genocide. And now, Beata had to figure out what to do – with her husband's body, with her three young children...with her life.

Through some family connections to the Rwandan military and the help of some friends who risked their lives for her, Beata was able to discretely recover the bodies, bring them to her in-laws' home, and prepare them for burial, which she did with the stoic determination and dissociated expertise that comes with being a nurse. Honestly, I cannot even comprehend the mental and emotional strength it took to do that. I cannot even imagine the pain, heartache, fear, anger, and need for justice that must have been tearing her apart. *Can you?*

With all of this churning inside her, Beata 'did what she had to do' and lovingly prepared the bodies for burial so that friends and family could help them have a proper, albeit rushed and fearful, funeral. Then, she gathered her children, a few belongings, and available funds so that they could attempt to flee their home, their families, and their country in order to survive. Their escape was not only incredibly difficult emotionally and physically, but also incredibly dangerous. It actually took three different attempts from multiple starting points and border-crossing routes over a six-week period of time, days and nights of living without shelter in the Nyungwe Forest, a lot of negotiation and pleading, a significant amount of 'safe passage' money, and finally a military escort for them to get out of Rwanda and into Burundi.

One of Beata's sisters had moved to the US several years earlier and was able to apply to bring Beata and her family there as refugees through the family reunification process. Beata did her part of the process through the US Embassy in Kenya, and after eight months, support from *Catholic Charities*, and the help of an entire network of people from all over the world who cared, this tragically widowed woman and her three young fatherless children were at least in a safe place to try to create a new life.

Beata realized that she had to start completely over and that she had to do that quickly. She learned English through an intensive course at a local learning center. Then, despite having a nursing degree and a graduate degree in public health, she needed to get her General Educational Development (GED) certificate because she could not access her transcripts from Rwanda. During this time, she took a job as a hotel cleaning lady, crying every day at work as she humbled herself to take care of her little family. She continued to build her new life by earning her Certified Nurse Assistant (CNA) certification and getting a higher paying and more enjoyable job in a nursing home. Over the next five years, Beata completed her (second) RN degree, built her own home through *Habitat for Humanity*, and became a US citizen. Unfortunately, her new life was not free from tragedy either - her son was killed in a car accident soon after he had finished college. Amazingly, she never let the pain, tragedy, and challenges define or deter her, but instead focused on the positives – surviving and escaping a genocide, help and support from so many individuals and organizations, a safe place to start over, opportunities, and hope. Her two daughters have embraced this positivity as well, the eldest completing MBA and Public Health Certification programs, now leading a medical research program at a prestigious children's hospital, and the youngest currently enrolled in medical school.

And Beata certainly did not want to just forget about Rwanda and erase all the horrifying and soul-crushing memories. Instead, she wanted to give back, help heal herself and others, and be part of rebuilding the safe and beautiful country that she grew up in. This is how I got to meet Beata and learn her story as we partnered with her to help rebuild her primary school in Butare, Rwanda. We ended up doing three projects at this school with Beata and learned so much from her and the other Rwandans about resilience, community, forgiveness, and hope.

During the second of these three projects, Beata took my wife, Cristi, and me to meet one of her friends who she had known since they were kids but had not seen since fleeing the country more than twenty years previously. After meeting the friend and five other acquaintances of similar age who had also survived the genocide by the grace of God, we sat down in the man's living room for tea and biscuits. They were very kind and genuine in asking us about our lives and our school-building organization and its mission, and listening to our stories. Then, the conversation shifted to them recounting their unfathomable and terrifying survival stories, the gut-wrenching and horrific stories of family members and friends who did not survive, and the truth and reconciliation and rebuilding efforts in Rwanda.

Cristi and I sat in respectful and rapt silence as these Rwandans gave very intense details about how, when, and where people they knew were killed, who had survived and where they now were, and who had taken part in the community gacaca courts and what the outcomes were. To us, it seemed heavy, cathartic, needed, and hopeful. There were many long silences while the reality and emotions hung over the circle of couches and chairs. There were no tears, but there was profound sorrow – for all Rwandans, for loss of life, for loss of innocence, for loss of opportunity. And then, there was a palpable and crescendoing transition to profound hope. It was unmistakable to us that this shared hope was rooted in the empathetic willingness to forgive. I was absolutely struck to my core and internally ripped apart by the dichotomy of knowing that forgiveness was the right thing to do while feeling that vengeance seemed like the only just and satisfying solution. Although it felt intrusive and awkward, I couldn't help myself in quietly and timidly making a self-incriminating statement that just seemed to float out into the room, "I cannot even imagine going through even the smallest part of what you have experienced and being willing to forgive anyone involved…"

After another respectful silence, Beata nodded her head several times, took a deep breath, and said, "I know from experience that it is very hard to forgive those who have killed your family member, but it is that reconciliation that will end hate faster than any court of justice can. To me, the future of Rwanda – and our world – lies in the hands of people who are willing to do that." Then, the tears fell – from everyone in the room – and I will never forget that moment and that feeling. **Beata taught me what real forgiveness means and the tremendous power that it holds – it is a power that we all can wield, and as she said, the only one that will end hate and bring a community, a country, and a world together.**

CHAPTER 12

LOVE—Jane (Momma)

Three things will last forever – faith, hope, and love – and the greatest of these is love.

~1 Corinthians 13:13 (NLT)

It was the first time I ever hesitated when I heard those words. I knew why I hesitated, and it was a stupid reason. I was seventeen years old and my two – very cute – high school classmates were listening. They didn't hear the words that made me hesitate, but they knew who I was on the phone with because I told them I needed to call her before we left. That's what made me hesitate...and it really was stupid of me.

Sometimes a sentence, a phrase, two words, even one word can change your life forever. In our first book, *Hand Delivered Hope*, we tell the story of how two words – *Books! Tuition!* – did just that. In that case, I only had to hear those two words one time from a group of desperately poor orphans in Zambia to set us on a lifelong journey to help build schools in the developing world. But the situation that I am referring to now, was many, many years earlier, it was three words, and actually, I literally heard them every single day of my life. And that is the point of this story.

The three words were from my Momma, who raised me and my three older sisters as a single parent with only a teacher's salary, more grit than a thousand of the toughest cowboys, and lots and lots of love. And, part of that love, was always thinking of others, including her 'baby boy.' She must have pictured the situation and realized why the hesitation occurred and so she said (with what I picture must have been a knowing smile on her face), "It's okay honey, you don't have to say..." but before she could finish, my heart overcame my foolish embarrassment, and I blurted out:

"I love you too, Momma!"

With a tiny quiver in her voice, she replied, "Thanks Tiger (my cherished nickname from her), have a good time with your friends!"

I hung up the phone (yes, a rotary dial land line) and turned around to see the two cute girls smiling that oh-aren't-you-just-adorable smile and my buddy Jon snickering like he just saw someone's pants fall down. But I guess I got the last laugh, because for the first full hour of the double date we then went on, both girls talked about how cute and sweet it was that I told my mom I loved her and how they wished they said and heard that more often. Even Jon agreed with that. Far more importantly, my Momma knew I really loved her and that I was even willing to 'tell the world' that I did – and then I could picture a contented and proud smile on her face and in her soul.

Ironically, I wrote this story down just two days before my Momma passed away from a sudden heart attack. If you knew my Momma, you knew love. If you didn't, I am sorry, because you truly missed out on a beautiful life-giving experience. She had such an easy, natural, authentic way of making you feel special just because you are you, she could light up a room with her smile because it came from a place and a source of true joy, and if you leaned into that with her, you were family, and she would do anything for family. She was the best encourager, advocate, cheerleader, celebrater, prayer warrior, and defender on the planet. She would figure out how to help you in any situation, usually before you knew what you needed, and do everything possible to make it happen. If you needed her for anything, anytime, anywhere, she would move heaven and earth for you. She was fierce. ***She wanted you to feel the love of our Father in heaven through His children here on earth – and man, was she ever great at that.***

Where did all that come from in her? Hope, kindness, generosity, compassion, humility, grit, courage, gratitude, empathy, joy, forgiveness, and love – modeled for her, taught to her, lived out for her, and then, ingrained in her so that she could send her own ripples out into the world. She weathered so many storms in her life – tragedies and heartaches that would break the strongest of humans – but she faced them all with grit and courage, and never ever lost hope. She practiced kindness, generosity, and compassion to people she didn't even know and to people she never even met. She taught my sisters and me to always be humble and thankful (and polite!). She modeled empathy and showed us how that allows you to forgive quickly. *And, oh my goodness, did she ever create joy in our lives!* We celebrated everything in our household - and I do mean celebrated! We literally had parades for getting baptized, parties for finishing big school assignments, shopping trips for reading books, special gifts for thoughtfulness, and special adventures for making new friends. And Christmas and birthdays – *don't get me started!* Now, don't get me wrong, Momma also believed strongly in disincentives, and we were absolutely held accountable for our actions, especially when they hurt others. But even the disincentives were delivered with love (albeit by way of a ruler, hairbrush, or wooden spoon) and always with an explanation, a lesson, and an application that helped you grow and learn. *What an incredible life she lived and what a beautiful legacy she left!*

I spent the weekend with her before she went to heaven. As always, she did all of the above (except the disincentives, thankfully). As I was leaving, having no idea that it would be the last time I saw her on this earth, I gave her a hug and a kiss, and said, *I love you, Momma!*

She said those three words one last time...without hesitating...

Epilogue

Each time a man stands up for an ideal, or acts to improve the lot of others, or strikes out against injustice, he sends forth a tiny ripple of hope, and crossing each other from a million different centers of energy and daring, those ripples build a current which can sweep down the mightiest walls of oppression and resistance.

~Robert F. Kennedy

Hope, kindness, generosity, compassion, humility, grit, courage, gratitude, empathy, joy, forgiveness, and love – I just want to let those beautiful waves wash over me again and again and again. And I want to reflect on how interconnected these character traits in action really are – each can make an individual splash, but then the ripples coincide and coalesce to make the total greater than the sum of its parts. In this way, the beautiful ripples you create come back to you as a full-fledged warm and soothing wave of inspiration to look for and find your light of hope and carry it with you as you use these powerful tools to change lives for the better.

I heard physician, activist, and author, Augustus White, say, "It doesn't have to be your fault in order to be your responsibility to try to make it better!" which synergizes with one of my favorite quotes from Mahatma Gandhi, "Be the change you wish to see in the world!" If we take these mission statements to heart and act upon them using the tools modeled by the life-changers in this book, we can certainly wash down the mightiest walls of oppression, injustice, prejudice, hatred, exclusion, indignity, and violence, and let everyone feel the warm waves of hope wash over them again and again and again.

So, I will challenge you to create ripples and make waves in the world each and every day – even if it causes some 'good trouble' (John Lewis). I am confident that, if accepted, this challenge will change many, many lives for the better, including your own.

CPSIA information can be obtained
at www.ICGtesting.com
Printed in the USA
BVHW061141021022
648491BV00003B/4